Table of Contents

1 Executive Summary of the Orchestration Systems 4

2 The Orchestration Problem 6

3 Competitive Analysis of the Orchestration Systems 7

 3.1 Selection Criteria 7

 3.2 Summary 8

4 The Adaptive Behavior Orchestration Solution 9

5 The Adaptive Behavior Orchestration Framework 11

 5.1 Language 11

 5.2 Domain Specific Models 11

 5.3 Policy Management Platform 11

  5.3.1 Policy User Interface & Wizards 12

  5.3.2 Policy Server 12

  5.3.3 Policy Engine 12

6 Baseline Version of the Adaptive Behavior Orchestration System 13

 6.1 Realization of Baseline Version 13

  6.1.1 Language 13

  6.1.2 Domain Specific Models 13

  6.1.3 Policy Management Platform 13

7 The Conclusion of the Adaptive Behavior Orchestration System 17

8 General Introduction of Video Surveillance Systems 18

 8.1 VidSys System Overview 18

 8.2 NICEVISION System Overview 19

 8.3 OnSSI 21

 8.4 Windows Workflow Foundation 22

9 Competitive Analysis of Video Surveillance Systems 24

 9.1 Enterprise Multimedia Fusion 24

 9.2 Enterprise Multimedia Managment 25

 9.3 Enterprise Security Managment 25

 9.4 Enterprise Architecture & Scalability 25

 9.5 Domain Analytics Capability 26

 9.6 Dynamic Business Process 26

 9.7 Adaptive Behavior Orchestration 26

 9.8 Policy Collision Detection, Validation and Distribution 27

 9.9 Other Limitations 27

  9.9.1 VidSys 27

  9.9.2 NICEVISION 28

9.9.3   OnSSI 28

9.9.4   Windows Workflow Foundation 28

10   Summary of Video Surveillance Systems 29

11   Appendix 31

   1.   Oracle 31

     1.1 Products 31

     1.2 Summary 32

   2. IBM 33

     2.1 Product 33

     2.2 Summary 34

   3. Red Hat 36

     3.1 Products 36

     3.2 Summary 37

   4. Microsoft 38

     4.1 Windows Workflow Foundation 38

     4.2 Summary 39

   5. TIBCO 40

     5.1 Products 40

     5.2 Summary 41

   6. Sun Microsystems 42

     6.1 Products 42

     6.2 Summary 43

   7. SAP 44

     7.1 Products 44

     7.2 Summary 45

   8. Fiorano 46

     8.1 Product 46

     8.2 Summary 47

   9. Lombardi 48

12   References 49

1 Executive Summary of the Orchestration Systems

The appeal of Business Process Management (BPM) lies not only in its highly embraced benefit of operational efficiency but also in its great promise of flexibility, agility, and adaptability to today's fast evolving businesses. Major advocates of BPM including IBM, Oracle, Sun, and SAP have expanded their BPM tools into an integrated set of offerings for process-managed enterprise solutions. These companies (and others) are more dedicated than ever to developing a flexible, integrated, and holistic BPM solution with advanced features to support business decisions and adapt to changing business needs. However, there are several challenging issues that are still open for investigation and require more research effort as follows.

- *Interoperability and scalability across diverse technologies* - The majority of the companies have adopted and supported BPEL4WS as the process modeling language and built their BPM systems around the WS standards. However, the integration of different process models in different languages with legacy functions across platforms and subsystems remains a challenging problem. All products have offered a centralized console for process management and control at the cost of scalability that is highly required in distributed environments.

- *Integration of process logic and decision logic* - Process logic and decision logic which are commonly intertwined within business processes are still being separated into two different management systems: the BPM system and the Business Rule Management (BRM) system, respectively. The use of rules to enable behavior orchestration has been limited to static workflow modeling and service selection.

- *Distributed decision making* - For distributed environments, decisions across all levels must be made automatically and coherently by multiple distributed parties that participate in composing or orchestrating services. The current centralized control paradigm employed by all offerings fails to address the distributed decision making problem.

Based on the above limitations of existing BPM solutions, a policy-based solution is proposed. As illustrated in Figure 3, this solution offers an extensible and pluggable policy framework that consists of:

1) A user interface (UI) for creating and modifying policies using the policy language
2) A policy server for analyzing, storing and distributing policies
3) A policy engine for executing and enforcing policies

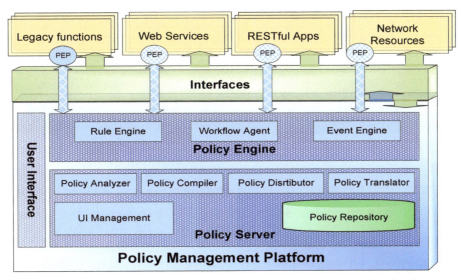

Figure 1: A policy-based solution for adaptive behavior orchestration

The policy-based solution aims to overcome the problems with existing BPM solutions mentioned above and enable adaptive behavior orchestration through the following offerings.

- A common language and a set of domain specific models to bridge the gap between business experts and IT professionals by unifying the different notations and models used for process modeling.
- The distributed Policy Enforcement Points (PEPs) incorporate the semantics of available functions, services, and sub-processes with syntactic interfaces to fully support interoperability and scalability and enable service composition and orchestration across legacy functions and newly created process models.
- The reactive nature of dynamic, policy-based process management improves flexibility and process automation by accommodating ad-hoc changes to the processes that are usually triggered by events.
- Distributed decision making not only provides intelligent decision making capabilities but also detects and resolves the policy conflicts between multiple parties that participate in service composition and/or orchestration.

The popular demand for flexibility and reliability has driven the Service Oriented Architecture (SOA) to a next wave of Event Driven-SOA (ED-SOA) and cloud computing that aim to decouple systems, services, and data from static processes and orchestrates them. For next generation enterprise systems (e.g., Rich media, Home gateway, etc.) that involve an increasing variety of autonomous stakeholders and their fragmented, distributed, and heterogeneous systems, policy-based adaptive behavior orchestration integrates process logic and decision logic to completely automate the dynamic assembly and coordination of services. Furthermore, by offering a fully distributed, scalable, and adaptable computing paradigm, the policy based solution can be easily adopted by existing software systems and enables future technologies such as ED-SOA and cloud computing.

2 The Orchestration Problem

The ultimate goal of process management is to provide sufficient flexibility to the users in process design and modeling and most importantly, allow the users to adapt their processes when needed. Although technologies such as SOA, web services, model-driven development, and workflow engines have gained growing attention and support, the major limitation of existing solutions for process management has always been the lack of support of adaptive behavior orchestration. Most of the proposed process management solutions either assume certain human experts (e.g. a business modeler with business knowledge and an IT person with programming knowledge) are responsible for the decision making that is involved in process design and management, or suppose that the processes are subject to very few changes, which is not true in current business environment with constant changes in service offerings, competitive landscape, markets, and regulations etc. The solutions fail to address the fact that for next generation systems, adaptive behavior orchestration is critical in order to support the flexibility and agility that is needed to handle unexpected changes with evolving business needs.

Another rudimentary fact is that most process models involve some form of decision making such as decision points, gateways, etc. Like the process itself, these decision making points are subject to changes as well. This further supports the need for automating the decision making in process management such as whether a pre-defined workflow is no longer adequate, or which changes of the original workflow definition have to be applied to better reflect the new situation. While most process management systems externalize the design and definition of control flow (for instance, business process management extracts out the flow of significant activities that are usually fulfilled by multiple heterogeneous subsystems or components), they all fail to provide effective means to coordinate and control the flows.

Previously proposed solutions including adaptive workflow, rule-based process management, and policy management in process modeling tackle the problem by using rules to capture and control the decision points in processes. Although the rule-based approach offers a practical solution for controlling processes, it is more effective in controlling the decision points for individual processes rather than coordinating the processes to change their collaborative behavior. In addition, rules in IF... THEN format are restrictive by their nature and limited in their expressive power. As a result, most existing rules engines can only handle propositional logic and first-order logic for the decision points within a process. They do not support modal logic that formalizes possibility, contingency, and necessity such as temporal logic (e.g. q will be true until a time when p is true) and deontic logic (e.g. it is forbidden that when p is true q is true) [1], which commonly exists in business processes.

3 Competitive Analysis of the Orchestration Systems

This section provides an analysis of the competition in the behavioral orchestration space. The main focus of this analysis is the ability of a competitor to accomplish dynamic workflow as described in previous sections. To provide a dynamic workflow product, there are some key elements that each competitor must provide. This analysis provides a description of their current capabilities and attempts to project what each company can provide within the next 24 months.

As shown in Table 1, the following components must exist to provide a dynamic workflow product:

1) Event mechanism (Events): Can events be used to trigger actions?
2) Rules Engine (Rules): Can rules be used to separate business logic?
3) Workflow Engine (Workflow): Can workflows be used to orchestrate
4) Enterprise Service Bus (ESB): Does a layer for distributed messaging exist?
5) Behavior Orchestration (Orchestration): Can their rules engine drive the workflow?

Company	Events	Rules	Workflow	ESB	Orchestration
Oracle	A	A	A	A	L
IBM	A	A	A	A	P, L
Red Hat	A	A	A	A	P
Microsoft	A	A	A	A	
TIBCO	A	A	A	A	L
Sun Microsystems	A		A	A	
SAP	A	A	A	A	
Fiorano	A		A	A	L
Lombardi		A	A	A	

Table 1: Criteria for competitive analysis (A = Available, P = Planned, L=Limited Support)

3.1 Selection Criteria

Although not an exact science, the companies that were selected for the competitive analysis were selected from 1 of 3 criteria. The first was to have entries in the BPM (Business Process Management), CEP (Complex Event Processing) and ESB (Enterprise Service Bus) columns in the summary chart in [2]. This lead to BEA Systems (now Oracle), Oracle, and TIBCO. IBM, Sun Microsystems, and Microsoft were also added because they had entries in some of the columns and are major software companies that could be competitors in this space.

The second was to be in the top percentages for BPMS Suites being used in [3] and to be a company that came up in previous searches. This led to SAP, and Lombardi being added to the list.

Finally, the third was subjective; the company either had to be a major software provider, a major open source provider or had to be a company that had come up in multiple searches. This led to Red Hat and

Fiorano being added to the list. For a detailed overview of each company involved in the analysis see Appendix.

3.2 Summary

We surveyed the competitive products in the above problem scope and examined the current capabilities and attempts to project what they can provide within the next 24 months. For a detailed list of the companies and their products, see Appendix.

Most companies have focused on the emerging needs of business process management in a SOA setting. Many of them have evolved around their core technology (e.g. IBM's ESB solutions, Oracle's Business Intelligence, etc.) and expanded their offerings by bringing BPM, BRM, and CEP together in an integrated set of SOA technologies. The active acquisitions in related BAM, BRM, and CEP markets by these companies have shown the growing needs and attractions in such offerings. More specifically, these companies have increased their efforts in the following areas:

- As evidenced by the key product features offered by the major players, the must-have capabilities of designing, automating, and improving the business processes have been greatly enhanced. All companies surveyed have offered built-in or separate process engines that allow the users to graphically model, deploy, monitor, and improve their business processes.

- All companies surveyed have developed ESB as a middleware solution that supports a generic set of functionality to enable communication, among which most companies provide general support of event processing and fault handling. Several companies (Oracle, IBM, Red Hat, and TIBCO) have included CEP in their event processing offerings to handle high volume, logically intricate, and semantically complex business events.

- The importance of service orchestration has been widely acknowledged. Although the support for behavior orchestration is still limited to web services and high-level business processes, we have witnessed successful applications of service selection, workflow improvement, and static service composition from companies like Oracle, Red Hat, IBM, TIBCO, and Fiorano.

- The other equally important new trend revealed by new offerings and/or future plans from many companies is the use of rules to automate decision making in process management. This includes Oracle's planned integration of business intelligence with BPEL PM, IBM's purchase and inevitable integration of ILOG BRMS, Microsoft's rule-based workflow engine, JBoss's plan of binding the Drools rules engine with the jBPM process engine, Lombardi's rules integration into workflows, and SAP's support of rules in process modeling.

4 The Adaptive Behavior Orchestration Solution

The use of policy provides an external and independent control point that can be leveraged to automate decision making through learning and reasoning for process management to realize adaptive behavior orchestration.

Before we describe the constituents of a policy based solution we first introduce the following essential concepts in the context of process management.

- Process: A formal/informal description of all the activities and their context as well as the decisions involved in the process from end to end in order to deliver a clear product or service to an external stakeholder or another internal process.
- Process Model: A formal representation that describes a process at the type level and thus a process is an instantiation of a process model.
- Workflow: A workflow is a reliably repeatable pattern of activity enabled by a systematic organization of resources, defined roles, and information flows, into a work process that can be documented, implemented, and executed. Workflows are the patterns that can be coordinated within processes whose instances are often subject to change and can be adapted to cope with a dynamic change and coordinated for behavior orchestration.
- Process management: Realizing the strategic objectives as well as the individual process goals through improvement, management, and control of the processes.
- Dynamic/Adaptive workflow: The adaptation of a workflow instantiation, usually during run-time, as a response to the changes that enable the workflow execution.
- Policy: Policies are defined from two perspectives:
  o A definite goal, course or method of action to guide and determine present and future decisions in managing the processes.
  o A set of rules to control, manage, and coordinate processes.
  Policies are implemented or executed within a particular context.

The policy-based solution aims to achieve adaptive behavior orchestration through dynamic workflow control (such as workflow selection and adaptation), dynamic workflow coordination (such as workflow creation and composition), and finally adaptive behavior orchestration across different technologies and subsystems. While goal-oriented policies and actionable rules define the desired system behavior and the corresponding course of actions, the decision making that is required to ensure the desired behavior as well as detect and resolve the conflict arising between different decisions depends on the learning and reasoning functionality provided by the policy-based solution.

The first step of a policy-based solution is to specify the policy, preferably in a generic business language. For systems with an Event-Driven Architecture (EDA), the policies are usually specified as Event-

Condition-Action (ECA) rules. The ECA type of policy considers the necessary actions that are triggered by changing contexts. Such reactive policies are best suited for event-centric problems that must respond to and manage the change. By specifying the behavioral context in events and conditions, that are inherent elements of a process, policy serves as a more natural and suitable form for representing and automating the decision making for dynamic process coordination and control.

After a policy is specified, the policy will be validated, compiled, stored, and distributed. The distribution of policies to components and/or subsystems makes the enforcement of policies not only flexible but also scalable by localizing the necessary decision making, all in the light of achieving the system goal. The conflicts between these distributed decisions are detected and resolved by the policy analyzer that is also responsible for validating the actions and amending the policies to guide and optimize the decisions to be made.

The Policy Enforcement Point (PEP), also named as the policy engine, is responsible for the dynamic execution of the policies. It further translates the policies into executable forms of actions and applies them to the corresponding decision points where the policies must be enforced.

5 The Adaptive Behavior Orchestration Framework

The policy-based solution for adaptive behavior orchestration is realized through a policy framework. A policy framework consists of multiple components, specifically: 1) a policy language specification; 2) domain specific models and 3) a Policy Management Platform.

5.1 Language

The Policy Language is used to specify the events conditions and actions that the system will use and is the payload that most components in the policy framework act upon.

5.2 Domain Specific Models

Every system has its own model that represents the knowledge in that system. In order for the Policy Framework to gain access to the system knowledge to create correct policies, the system's model must be made available. The models will provide the facts for the language and framework to reference.

5.3 Policy Management Platform

As shown in Figure 2, the policy management platform consists of three major components: the user interface and wizards (UI), the policy server, and the policy engine.

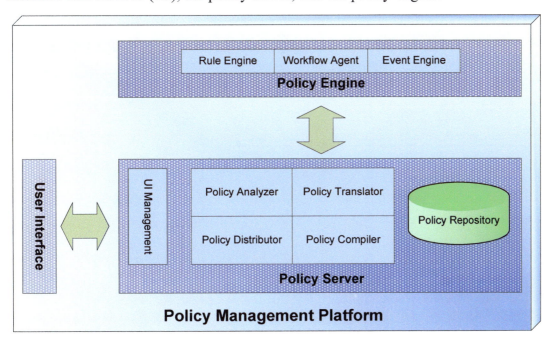

Figure 2: Policy Management Platform

The user interface and wizards provide the user with a set of informative and intuitive means to specify policies. The policy server interacts with the UI and the policy engine to process, analyze, translate, compile, store, and provide access to the policies. The policy engine contains three main components: an event engine, a rules engine, and a workflow agent. The components process the events, the underlying logic and reasoning, and the actions in the form of workflows, respectively. The policy engine also includes a set of pluggable agents that interfaces with different communication channels to detect actionable events and distribute corresponding actions that need to be taken as specified by policies.

5.3.1 Policy User Interface & Wizards

The Policy User Interface and Wizards are a set of tools (IDEs, Compilers, etc.) that are linked to the models and allow the business users to create, store, manage and deploy policies.

5.3.2 Policy Server

The Policy Server primarily functions as the policy storage point and the policy distribution point. The Policy Server co-ordinates with the UI and stores the policies in the Policy Repository. It also analyzes, translates, compiles and distributes the policies to the Policy Engines. The Policy Server has the following components, UI Manager, Policy Analyzer, Policy Repository, Policy Translator, Policy Compiler and the Policy Distributor.

5.3.3 Policy Engine

The Policy Engine processes and executes the Policies. The Policy Engine consists of an Event Engine, a Rules Engine and a Workflow Agent. It also contains a set of pluggable components for interfacing with the native system. The Policy Engine listens for events from the system and determines which policies to execute based on the context of the detected event. After executing these policies the Policy Engine enforces the required actions on the native system.

6 Baseline Version of the Adaptive Behavior Orchestration System

The purpose of the baseline version (version 0) is to realize distributed policy for dynamic workflow by demonstrating dynamic selection of static workflows using policy. Basically, a policy is used to specify the triggers (events) the context (conditions) and the corresponding workflows to execute (actions). Depending on the state of a system or subsystem, a certain workflow will be executed.

6.1 Realization of Baseline Version

Below are the changes that are needed for the baseline version.

6.1.1 Language

The existing policy language [4] can be largely reused without modification to support the specification of ECA policy rules. However, the language will minimally need to be extended to support workflows.

6.1.2 Domain Specific Models

The language will need to reference the same models that exist in the workflow and rules engines. A mechanism will need to exist to allow for the domain specific models to be referenced by the language. The internal domain model of the policy framework will also need to be modified to minimally allow for workflows and processes. There might be significant work on the internal model.

6.1.3 Policy Management Platform

Below are some of the design considerations for the policy management platform:
1. Use of commercial off the shelf (COTS) components/products
2. Pre-compiling Policies for faster execution at the Policy Execution Point (PEP)
3. Memory footprint of the Policy Engine
4. CPU requirements for running the Policy Engine.
5. Interfacing capabilities to talk to external systems.
6. Interfacing capabilities to interact with external processes, workflows, etc.

To focus on solving behavioral orchestration problems, the framework should be redesigned to utilize existing COTS components and products, specifically COTS rule and workflow engines.

COTS components and products are fairly mature and provide pieces that can be leveraged with minimal changes. However, in order to use a COTS rules engine we need to take into consideration most do not support events, only conditions and actions. Enabling policy rules which contain events along with conditions and actions to use a COTS rules engine, requires a policy rule to be broken down into an event portion and a condition-action portion and processed separately.

A rules engine will be bundled with other components to compose a policy engine that is responsible for processing policies specified by a business user. A workflow engine must be in place in order to implement and execute the workflows, and a workflow agent must interact with the workflow engine.

The subsystems of the baseline version 0 of the Policy Management Platform are described in more detail below. The sections also outline the changes that are required to be made to the current version on the Policy Management Platform to get to version 0 described in this document.

6.1.3.1 Policy User Interface & Wizards

The Policy User Interface and Wizards (UI) is a set of Web-based tools (IDEs, Parser, etc) that allow the users to build, store, manage and apply policies on the system. The Web-based interface allows the tools to be used any operating system, with no special software to be deployed. The tools are built using AJAX, which provides a superior user experience. The UI interact with the Policy Server to store and distribute policies to various subsystems.

Changes in the UI and Wizards:
1. A UI for distributing policies and applying policies to the various subsystems is required.
2. UI for analyzing policies and eventually showing the results of conflict detection and providing resolutions.

6.1.3.2 Policy Server

The Policy Server stores, analyzes, pre-processes and distributes the policies. It interfaces with both the UI and the Policy Engines on various subsystems. The Policy Server consists of the following components:
1. UI Session Manager: This component interfaces with the Policy Management UI. It receives Policies to be stored from the UI and stores it in the Policy Repository using the Policy Repository Service.
2. Policy Repository Service: This is a service interface to the Policy Repository. Any component that needs information from the Policy Repository will access it using the Policy Repository Service. The Policy Repository Service provides database query services as well as other convenience services.
3. Policy Repository: All the Policy information is stored in the Policy Repository. Besides the ECA Policy Rules, this repository can also store translated policies (translated by the Policy Translator) and the compiled Policy Objects (compiled by the Policy Event Compiler and/or a Rules compiler). All access to the Policy Repository is via the Policy Repository Service.
4. Policy Analyzer: The Policy Analyzer analyzes the policies to reason about the policies and the related decision points and detects conflicts in the policies. This component will be the result of the research on Policy Conflict Detection and Resolution.

5. Policy Translator: This component is required for translating the ECA Policy Rules into the Policy Event components and Policy Condition-Action components as described above. The Policy Translator component may either be part of the Policy Server or the Policy Engine itself, depending on the deployment requirements. The Policy Translator may also map the our Policy text to form required by the COTS Rules Engine.

6. Policy Compiler: This component is used to compiling the translated Policies from the Policy Translator into a form that can be executed on the Policy Engine (Event Engine and Rules Engine). This component can belong to either the Policy Server or the Policy Engine. This component may also store the compiled form in the Policy Repository for future use.

7. Policy Distributor: The Policy Distributor is an agent that distributes or sends the Policies to the Policy Engines on various subsystems. This component supports both a push and a pull paradigm. A Policy Engine can either contact the Policy Distributor for updates or new Policies or the Policy Distributor can push updates or new Policies to Policy Engines on the system.

Changes to the Policy Server:

1. Policy UI Session Manager: The UI Session Manager will add extra interfaces for Policy Distribution UI and Policy Analyzer UI (if needed)

2. Policy Repository Service: The current version of the Policy Repository Server needs to be updated to provide more convenience functions. Also, depending on the requirements, the Policy Repository and the Policy Repository Service may need to be changed to store translated and compiled policies if required.

3. Policy Analyzer: A Policy Analyzer needs to be added to the current system. This component may or may not be added depending on whether conflict detection is a requirement or not.

4. Policy Translator: A Policy Translator component will need to be implemented for version 0.

5. Policy Compiler: Minimally, a Policy Compiler for compiling the Policy Events will need to be implemented for version 0. For the Policy Condition-Action rules, we can use the compilers available in the COTS Rules Engine.

6. Policy Distributor: The current version of the Policy Distributor needs to be updated to support both push and pull paradigms. The current version supports the push paradigm.

6.1.3.3 Policy Engine

The Policy Engine consists of the following components:

1. Event Engine: The Event Engine processes the compiled Policy Event objects. It listens for events on the sensor interface and determines which PCA rules should be fired in the rules engine based on the type/name of the event received.

2. Rules Engine: This component processes the compiled PCA rules. On receiving information from the event engine regarding which rule(s) should be fired, the rules engine executes the corresponding rules. It evaluates the conditions specified in the rule(s) and takes the

corresponding actions depending on the result of the evaluation. The Rules Engine uses the Sensor Effector pair as the interface for evaluating conditions and executing actions.

3. Policy Translator and Policy Compiler: Depending on the requirements these components (described above) can also be part of the Policy Engine.

4. Workflow Agent: The Workflow Agent allows the Policy Engine to interface with a Workflow engine, thus allowing the Actions specified in the Policies to trigger different Workflows and enable orchestration.

5. Sensor and Effector interfaces: The Policy Engine also has a number of Sensor and Effector interfaces to allow it to interface with other systems for getting information and also enforcing actions on these systems.

Changes to the Policy Engine:

1. An Event Engine needs to be implemented for the Policy Engine.

2. Rules Engine: Although a COTS Rules Engine will be adopted for version 0, some work needs to be done to interface the Rules Engine with the Sensors and Effectors. In addition, the Rules Engine must be able to interface with the Event Engine.

3. Workflow Agent: A Workflow Agent to interface with a Workflow Engine needs to be implemented.

4. Sensors and Effectors: In order to interface with more subsystems, more Sensors and Effectors need to be implemented.

7 The Conclusion of the Adaptive Behavior Orchestration System

Next generation enterprise solutions promise to deliver demand driven, integrated, and personalized services through dynamic service creation and orchestration. BPM and its related offerings that aim to achieve service orchestration have received growing attention with the advances of SOA technologies. However, our competitive survey shows that due to their centralized, web-based orchestration design, existing products do not provide the flexibility and interoperability required in dynamic assembly and coordination of services, which commonly involve massively distributed components, legacy systems, and diverse technologies. Moreover, none of the current solutions fully integrate process logic with decision logic. Nor do they take into account the local autonomies and address the need for distributed decision making in service composition and orchestration.

Policy-based adaptive behavior orchestration is proposed to tackle these problems and provide a fully distributed and scalable solution. It is designed to offer an extensible and pluggable framework with an external and independent control point, allowing distributed decision making to be completely automated and integrated with process management. We embark on the policy management platform development by first offering a baseline solution for policy based dynamic workflow selection across legacy functions and web services. We will further advance this solution by adding support to dynamic workflow coordination and control. As a parallel research effort, distributed intelligent decision support and conflict detection and resolution will also be addressed. At last, we envision the policy based solution to be integrated into next generation service delivery platforms for emerging businesses. The research is currently underway.

8 General Introduction of Video Surveillance Systems

The study is intended to review and describe the existing technologies for General & Public Safety (G&PS) Initiative, and provides the analysis on the competitive situation. It covers the overview of the market players, overview of their limitations, identification and assessment of different options to increase competition.

8.1 VidSys System Overview

VidSys offers two software solutions, VidShield for video management and RiskShield for situation management. Both offerings are based on its Open Physical Security Information Management (PSIM) software platform that integrates security device management with certain capabilities of intelligent computing. The PSIM is designed for configuring and connecting various devices to collect security information from multiple sources in real-time, with a strong focus on video content. The PSIM contains four engines to process the gathered information and present the necessary data to VidShield and RiskShield:

- *Rules Engine:* Analyzes events and mainly supports event filtering and event correlation based on certain rules/policies;
- *Routing Engine:* Supports distributed routing by identifying sources and destinations of information and optimizing the routes for transferring the data;
- *Geospatial Engine:* Provides spatial recognition for geo-location of devices and supports situation mapping functionality; and
- *Dispatch Engine:* Interacts with communication infrastructure to distribute information such as messages, data and commands.

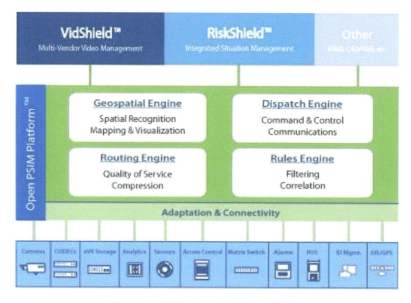

Figure 3: VidSys System Overview

8.2 NICEVISION System Overview

NICEVision integrates real-time video analytics, IP networking, recording and management to enable automatic threat detection, instant verification, event resolution and effective investigation.

NICEVision Systems has identified the *Intelligent Security Cycle*, a proactive, systematic approach to managing security and improving performance. Highly effective security teams use video surveillance to accelerate five primary activities in the security process:

- *Detection:* Detect threats automatically using video content analytics
- *Verification:* Automatically provide context information to enable rapid verification of events by instant replay (which shows how the event occurred) and live video (which shows precisely what is happening now).
- *Event Resolution:* Empower the event resolution process with automation and structure: the NICEVision video management system sends alerts to the person who needs to know about them, provides relevant task lists, and helps teams coordinate to better handle the situation.
- *Investigation:* Accelerate investigations by prioritizing content-based video footage
- *Continuous Improvement:* Improve security operations with advanced reports, graphs and applications.

NICEVision product families include the following components:

- *NICEVision ControlCenter:* A suite of fully integrated software applications providing easy-to-use and highly flexible management tools for controlling the most demanding multi-site video surveillance operations. It helps operators detect, verify, resolve and investigate security events quickly and effectively.
  a) *Virtual video matrix (VMX):* Combines analog matrix functionality with advanced event management; enables one to control any camera from any authorized workstation or CCTV keyboard, and display any camera on any monitor, anywhere on the network.
  b) *PDA solution:* Enables security on the move
  c) *Central Database:* Configure every aspect of widely distributed or single-site operations from any location on the network via a secure centralized database
  d) *Web interface:* Easy installation and launch of the control application that supports widely distributed teams or large numbers of operators
  e) *Software development kit (SDK):* Provides all the tools needed to link powerful IP video management with other security and information systems.
     - Exchange data and events with other systems
     - Embed live and replayed video in other systems
     - Comprehensive API and ActiveX components provide complete access to NICEVision functionality

- *NICEVision Net:* A complete, end-to-end IP video surveillance solution that includes intelligent edge devices with built-in analytics, network video recorders/encoders/decoders, video content analytics, extensive event management, and control room visualization.

- *NICEVision Analytics:* A portfolio of field-proven video content analytics applications, which includes intrusion detection, vehicle detection, unattended baggage detection, pICEle counting, and counter-flow detection module. NiceVision Analytics is integrated with the NICEVision ControlCenter management application, providing important decision-making information, leveraging its inherent real-time recording and review capabilities, and data-driven access for enhanced scenario reconstruction.

- *NiceVision Digital:* A family of Digital Video Recorders (DVRs) that provides a variety of solutions for different channel capacity and site requirements:
  a) *NiceVision PRO:* Combines high video quality, massive digital recording and advanced video networking in delivering the most comprehensive security solution for better security operation.
  b) *NiceVision ALTO:* A versatile solution for digital video and audio recording, analysis and management, designed for the mid to high-end security market.
  c) *NiceVision NVSAT:* A smart video CODEC for encoding and streaming high-quality video over IP networks, as well as performing real-time distributed video analysis.

- *FAST alpha silver Encoders/Codecs:* IP-based MPEG-2 and MPEG-4 video and audio recording solution

Figure 4: NICEVISION System Overview

8.3 OnSSI

OnSSI, On-Net Surveillance Systems, Inc., develops a non-proprietary, open architecture, management platform. Ocularis is the term OnSSI is using for its entire platform – NVRs, client software, plugins, etc.

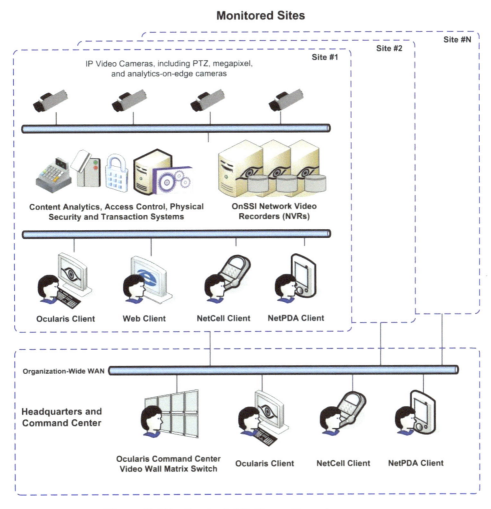

Figure 5: The Ocularis Platform Overview

According to OnSSI, the three most significant differentiators of Ocularis are:

- Ease of use: Whereas most IP video surveillance applications are fairly cumbersome, the Ocularis client is very ease to use for the non-expert user typical in security.
- Openness to support 3rd party DVR/NVR/IP Video Surveillance software. Ocularis is designed to work not only with OnSSI's recorders but with other manufacturers. Given that many large organizations need to maintain multiple manufacturer's systems, this provides not only an easy to use client application but a singular application across all video systems.
- Ocularis Client Lite interface is provided with OnSSI recorders.

Ocularis Client is an application that operators and investigators use to monitor and respond to security events. It is a thick client, not a web application, and must be installed on each user's PC. Ocularis Client is a separate application and communicates with recorders over an IP network (OnSSI's own recorders or others). It retrieves video from those recorders and then presents them in ways that are novel for video surveillance (novel for UI representation).

OnSSI advertises two main features as being their strength in the client, touch screen and time slicing The time slicing feature enables immediate access to recorded events. Automatically generated time-interval thumbnails allow drilling down in time to identify the exact moment an event occurred. In a matter of seconds you can access the moment of the event, apply digital PTZ and motion detection, export a video clip and distribute it to law enforcement and other users.

The video content analytics modules provide automated detection of events, objects and behaviors. Content analytics can be applied to both live and recorded video, with multiple detectors and unlimited detection rules per camera, and interoperability with analytics on edge devices. On-event push video alerts can be automatically or manually pushed to designated alert views, from which they can be further investigated and exported as evidence. By receiving filtered video, fewer operators are needed to monitor a far greater number of locations. Ocularis offers a wide array of unique investigation tools. Camera views transition between playback and live monitoring, and can be investigated using optical PTZ, as well as digital PTZ, into both live and recorded video by drawing a square on the desired object or area.

Compared to most IP video surveillance software providers, OnSSI recorders support a very broad range of IP cameras as well as features, functionalities and 3rd party integrations. OnSSI offers multiple tiers of software levels with various functions at different pricing:

- NetDVMS: Enterprise class software solution from ONSSI supports hundreds of cameras. This is ideal for multi-site applications, and provides centralized command and control of multiple locations.
- NetDVR: This is midrange software solution from ONSSI with many features that are similar to NetDVMS. It is a single server application that supports up to 64 cameras.
- ProSight: System for small business and home applications from ONSSI with many similar features to NetDVR. Supports up to 25 cameras

8.4 Windows Workflow Foundation

Windows Workflow Foundation (WF) is a Microsoft technology for defining, executing, and managing workflows. This technology was first released in November 2006 as part of the .NET Framework 3.0. Microsoft has indicated that workflows are going to be a cornerstone of their future Service Oriented Architecture platform. WF provides .NET developers with the ability to separate the logic of their application from the underlying execution components, thus providing a clearer, more manageable representation of the application. This approach lends credence to the growing process-driven application methodology, which aims to separate an application's logical flow from its executable components at an enterprise level.

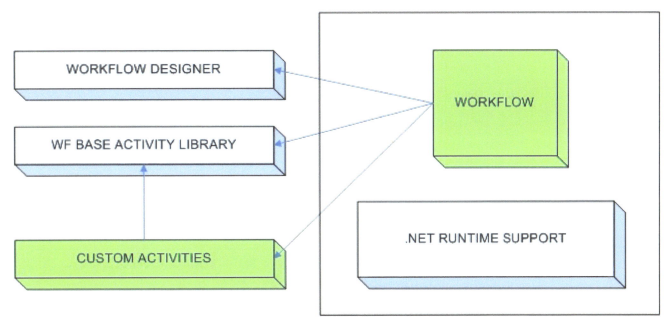

Figure 6: WF Architecture Overview

Workflows comprise of 'activities'. Developers can write their own domain-specific activities and then use them in workflows. WF also provides a set of general-purpose 'activities' that cover several control flow constructs. Windows Workflow Foundation is supported by a companion set of extensions to Visual Studio 2005. These extensions contain a visual workflow designer which allows users to design workflows, a visual debugger which enables the users to debug the workflow designed, and a project system which enables the user to compile their workflows inside Visual Studio 2005. In Visual Studio 2008 WF functionality is included.

WF provides several ways to communicate with a running instance of a Workflow:

- A Windows Communication Foundation approach to workflow communication was added in .NET Framework 3.5. Workflows which include a ReceiveActivity expose a selected interface method as a WCF service. This could allow external code to, for example, make a Web Services call to a running workflow instance. WF provides infrastructure to ensure that if a WCF call is made to a workflow instance that is idle (i.e. waiting for some external event like a WCF call or a timer event), then the instance will be loaded from storage into memory so that the message can be delivered. Workflows which include a SendActivity are, in turn, able to call external services via WCF.

- When a workflow instance is created, the host application can provide information in Dictionary objects. Similarly, the Workflow can pass the results of the workflow to the Host application through a Dictionary Object.

- The Workflow foundation also allows the Workflow to update the Host application of the progress of the workflow. This is done by raising events in the Workflow to which the host application will subscribe.

Using the WF foundation, three different types of Workflow can be created:

- Sequential Workflow (Typically Flow Chart based, progresses from one stage to next and does not step back)
- State Machine Workflow (Progress from 'State' to 'State', these workflows are more complex and return to a previous point if required)
- Rules-driven Workflow (Implemented based on Sequential/StateMachine workflow. The rules dictate the progress of the workflow)

The .NET Framework 3.0/3.5 "workflow runtime" provides common facilities for running and managing the workflows and can be hosted in any CLR application domain, be it a Windows Service, a Console, GUI or Web Application. The host can provide services like serialization for the runtime to use when needed. It can also hook up to workflow instance's events such as their becoming idle or stopping.

9   Competitive Analysis of Video Surveillance Systems

This section provides specific details about some of the limitations found in the surveyed products. Table 2 is a summary of the functionality per product.

Company / Item	VidSys	NICE	OnSSI	WF
Enterprise Multimedia Fusion	3	3	3	1
Enterprise Multimedia Management	3	3	3	1
Enterprise Security Management	1	1	1	3
Enterprise Architecture & Scalability	3	3	3	4
Domain Analytics Capability	2	4	3	0
Dynamic Business Process	2	1	1	3
Adaptive Behavior Orchestration	1	1	1	3
Policy Collision Detection, Validation and Distribution	0	0	0	2

Table 2: Criteria for competitive analysis

(5 = Fully, 4 = Partial, 3 = Limited, 2 = Very Limited, 1 = Unlikely, 0 = Not available)

9.1 Enterprise Multimedia Fusion

A multimedia fusion framework can provide an underlying architecture and information pool that applications can leverage for system commonality. It also can scale for new services, substantial multimedia management, ingestion, and streaming capacity for large-scale sources.

The multimedia framework should be able to encompass the close linkage of Metadata tags applied to multimedia, Policy, and Security. It should be able to orchestrate services among separate systems to enable communication & sharing of data. Finally, it should be able to support converged multimedia for devices, vehicle and dispatch environments, while considering roles & workflow.

9.2 Enterprise Multimedia Managment

Public safety does need a system for multimedia information (textual, audio, speech, image, and video) management. It should be able to collect media from various devices in the system and ingest the metadata into a common data model that supports inter-content relationships; it should be able to provide timely, salient, & actionable multimedia incident information (key content items, incident summaries, alerts, and alarms) for relevant public safety workers to use in both mid-incident and post-incident use cases; it should be able to retrieve textual, audio, speech, image, and video content to provide efficient, comprehensive, and combined retrieval through queries of metadata describing content or content directly; it should be able to analyze, aggregate and distribute multiple media sources in a way that provides new knowledge and makes it immediately actionable.

9.3 Enterprise Security Managment

It is essential to provide the enterprise security management such as role based access control to multi-media, and group management. Enterprise security management should be able to provide managed access for appropriate time periods to authorized users/roles. For example, it will allow a police office responding to an incident to have access to camera feeds from a bank, prevent non law enforcement from accessing same information, block access to non involved law enforcement, or terminate the access after the incident. It should be able to form and manage access control for groups for incident areas, and provide the ability for groups to be composed and managed during emergency situations such as quickly creating groups, adding or modifying members, removing groups and crossing agency devices/personnel to be included in such a process.

9.4 Enterprise Architecture & Scalability

The demand for flexibility and reliability of systems requires architectures to support policy based dynamic workflow. Without such an architecture such as a Service Oriented Architecture (SOA) and Event Driven-SOA (ED-SOA), it becomes difficult to decouple systems, services, and data from static processes and orchestrate them,. Furthermore, without such an architecture, it cannot offer a fully distributed, scalable, and adaptable computing paradigm, a policy based solution cannot be easily adopted by existing software systems and cannot enable future technologies such as cloud computing.

The current centralized control paradigm employed by all offerings fails to address the distributed decision making problem. For distributed environments, decisions across all levels must be made automatically and coherently by multiple distributed parties that participate in composing or orchestrating services. There is no policy server for analyzing, storing and distributing policies, and incorporating the semantics of available functions, services, and sub-processes with syntactic interfaces to fully support interoperability and scalability and enable service composition and orchestration across legacy functions and newly created process models.

9.5 Domain Analytics Capability

Public safety produces much more content than ever before due to increasingly larger systems. NICE, OnSSI, VidSys all have limited video content analytics. NiceVision Analytics is a portfolio of field-proven video content analytics applications, which includes intrusion detection, vehicle detection, unattended baggage detection, people counting, and the new counter-flow detection module. It is integrated with the NiceVision ControlCenter management application, providing important decision-making information. OnSSI provides Content Analytics modules that enable efficient automation of event detection, analysis, management processes, and detecting behavior patterns for motion and non-motion corresponding. VidSys RiskShield provides situation management, auditing capabilities, and tracking functionality. VidSys partners with Vidient, ObjectVideo, and OnSSI to enhance its analytics capability.

9.6 Dynamic Business Process

Business process lies not only in its highly embraced benefit of operational efficiency but also in its great promise of flexibility, agility, and adaptability to today's fast evolving businesses. There should be a combination of process and decision logic management, which are commonly intertwined within business processes. The use of rules to enable behavior orchestration has been limited to static workflow modeling and service selection. There is no dynamic, policy-based process management.

9.7 Adaptive Behavior Orchestration

The assumption that certain human experts are responsible for the decision making that is involved in process design and management will not provide sufficient flexibility to the users in process design and modeling and most importantly, allowing the systems and users to adapt their processes when needed.

If we externalize the design and definition of control flow, that will fail to provide effective means to coordinate and control the flows. Most process models involve some form of decision making such as decision points, gateways, etc. Like the process itself, these decision-making points are subject to changes as well. This further supports the need for automating the decision-making in process management such as whether a pre-defined workflow is no longer adequate, or which changes of the original workflow definition have to be applied to better reflect the new situation.

Most of the products do not support modal logic that formalizes possibility, contingency, and necessity such as temporal logic (e.g. q will be true until a time when p is true) and deontic logic (e.g. it is forbidden that when p is true q is true), which commonly exists in business processes. They cannot achieve adaptive behavior orchestration as there is no dynamic workflow control (such as workflow selection and adaptation), dynamic workflow coordination (such as workflow creation and composition), and adaptive behavior orchestration across different technologies and subsystems.

9.8 Policy Collision Detection, Validation and Distribution

There is no detection and resolution for the policy conflicts between multiple parties that participate in service composition and/or orchestration. There also does not appear to be a plan for this in any of the surveyed products. They do not have the mechanism to validate and distribute rules/policies. The distribution of policies to components and/or subsystems makes the enforcement of policies not only flexible but also scalable by localizing the necessary decision-making, all in the light of achieving the system goal. The conflicts between these distributed decisions are detected and resolved by the policy analyzer that is also responsible for validating the actions and amending the policies to guide and optimize the decisions to be made.

9.9 Other Limitations

9.9.1 VidSys

VidSys offers a leading solution in the multi-media security information management space because of its abilities to manage large amount of video contents from various sources in real-time to support video analysis and more advanced applications such as situation resolution. The most compelling video management feature of VidSys is its advanced video processing functions including visualization, tracking, geo-spatial mapping, etc., which are all supported by the underlying engines embedded in its PSIM platform. VidSys greatly benefits from its platform architecture. By building an integration platform with certain computational intelligence embedded for specific domains (e.g. video management and situation resolution), the development of advanced management applications and services can be decoupled from the communication infrastructure. VidSys offers a rules engine, which is centralized for all rules management and control at the cost of scalability that is highly required in distributed environments. However, the dependency on the platform and its integrated and centralized information processing and analytics capabilities also limits the extensibility and scalability of the applications that can only be built on top of the platform. John Honovich, the founder of IP Video Market Info, pointed out that VidSys PSIM has major structural problems that may limit its utility to the very largest security organizations, including serious operational limitations and deployment complexities from operational, interoperability, performance and pricing issues.

Although four engines have been developed for intelligent information processing, their functionalities are disjoint and confined by the information each one of them is designed to process. The importance of situation awareness is not reflected in these engines and there is a lack of intelligence automation and a strong dependency of pre-loaded expertise to enable the information analyses. In other words, all the engines are driven by certain types of information and act passively to process such information for specific applications. The ability to proactively gather, move, analyze, and dispatch necessary information that is driven by situations is not supported.

9.9.2 NICEVISION

NICEVision provides a powerful end-to-end video surveillance solution. NiceVision ControlCenter seamlessly manages the complete range of NiceVision network video recorders (NVRs), IP edge devices, DVRs and video analytics, as well as integrating with third party security and information systems (via its SDK). Also, it can control and display video from any third party IP device on any console. However, its current analytics functionality is limited to a few aspects that are specific to certain scenarios (e.g, intrusion detection, vehicle detection, unattended baggage detection, people counting, and counter-flow detection module). NICEVISION offers a leading solution in analytics. But it does not have any rule/policy engine, which greatly limits its scalability and flexibility that is highly required in distributed environments. The dependency on the closed platform and closed information processing and analytics capabilities limits the extensibility and scalability of the applications that can only be built on top of them.

9.9.3 OnSSI

OnSSI Software is non-proprietary, open architecture. It delivers camera management, recording and archiving, and automated video alerts based on analysis and detection. Ocularis client uses the latest version of Microsoft's graphical subsystem, the Direct 3D. This is important because it allows OnSSI to implement advanced functionalities that are not feasible in the framework that most other vendor's use - WinForms. OnSSI has not announced what 3rd party recorders they will be supporting.

However, its analysis capability strongly depends on pre-loaded expertise to enable the information analyses. This will pretend them to proactively gather, move, analyze, and dispatch necessary information that is driven by events/situations/service orchestration. Plus, in distributed environments, without SOA/ED-SOA architecture, any event management engine, and any rule/policy engine, its scalability and flexibility limitation is greatly high. That also limits the extensibility and scalability of its platform.

9.9.4 Windows Workflow Foundation

Microsoft WF does provide both a workflow engine and rules engine. The rules engine can be separate from the workflow engine and use business rules to control workflow. However, it only has limited dynamic workflow management capability. First, it is not event-driven business rule management. The rules are only evaluated at fixed points when the workflow reaches the pre-set activity point. Second, the workflow can not be dynamically composed. While policies can be changed and re-evaluated, the branches of workflows are pre-established and can't be changed at runtime. And WF Rule engine does not put emphasis on policy conflict detection but just mention priority value to remove conflict.

10 Summary of Video Surveillance Systems

Current products do not provide the flexibility and interoperability required in dynamic assembly and coordination of services, which commonly involve massively distributed components, legacy systems, and diverse technologies. Moreover, none of them fully integrates process logic with decision logic. Nor do they take into account the local autonomies and address the need for distributed decision making in service composition and orchestration. The demand for the system is to deliver demand driven, integrated, and personalized services through dynamic service creation and orchestration.

What we can offer is a multimedia fusion framework with service coordination and orchestration capabilities, not only for services that are built on top of the platform but also for 3rd party services, applications, as well as legacy functions, with a coherent set of analytical functions to fully support automated and scalable decision making capabilities (i.e., through the government of dynamic, situation-aware policies):

- *A Single Unified Platform:* The unified process offers a ubiquitous, service oriented solution for public security system across all public security domains. Unified SOA and business process management makes all integration modules participate in end-to-end governance and management through integration with multimedia repository and SOA Management. Its integration seamlessly integrates with multimedia to service-enable public security business processes to be flexible enough to meet the evolving demands of requirements.
- *Multimedia Fusion:* The multimedia data services management platform is for building Information-as-a-Service (IaaS) deployments. It transforms heterogeneous, siloed multimedia data into reusable information services providing real-time, accurate information to people, processes, and applications. It also includes technology for the complete information-services life cycle, including ingestion, archiving, indexing, analysis, retrieval, dispatch, and management.
- *Dynamic Service Orchestration:* Public security organizations need to leverage the existing applications, but also expand their capabilities by transforming them into services in order to drive new levels of customer service and move quickly into dynamic situations/environments. They need services distributed across multiple public security domains to build high-value composite applications. The integration framework unifies and simplifies their efforts to integrate all systems, applications, and data sources to get tangible results. It ensures investment protection in existing applications and infrastructure now and into the future.
- *Security Management:* Let only the right people to access the right information in the right place at the right time.

A policy-based adaptive behavior orchestration solution can be used to tackle these problems and provide a fully distributed and scalable solution. It is designed to offer an extensible and pluggable framework with an external and independent control point, allowing distributed decision making to be completely automated and integrated with process management.

11 Appendix

Below is a detailed overview for each company involved in the competitive analysis (Section 3).

1. Oracle

Through multiple acquisitions Oracle has quickly graduated to become one of the world's largest enterprise software companies. Oracle's Fusion Middleware solution, now bolstered with the acquisition of BEA Weblogic, provides it all the components needed to provide end-to-end, SOA, enterprise application integration (EAI) and service delivery platform (SDP) solutions. With respect to providing a product that can do dynamic workflow orchestration, Oracle has all the products/components needed to provide a solution in less than 24 months. The only question is whether it's in their roadmap.

1.1 Products

1) Events: Oracle first built event processing into their fusion middleware in 2004 primarily for Business Activity Monitoring (BAM). This graduated into a full blown event drive application (EDA) Suite, which included: (i) event processing, (ii) enterprise messaging, (iii) an ESB and (iv) a Rules Engine for processing business events.

   Oracle also has a Complex Event Processor (CEP) for high-throughput stream processing, event correlation and detection, and pattern style matching. The CEP is part of their middleware suite and can be fully integrated with their application server. At this time I am not aware of any standards for CEP and do not know if Oracle adheres to any.

2) Rules: As part of their Fusion Middleware stack, Oracle has a full blown Business Rules product that includes a Business Rules Engine, a Business Rules Language, a Rules SDK and a Business Rules Rule Author. The Rules Engine and processing is based on the Rete algorithm and is also capable of doing Complex Event Processing. Oracles Rules Engine is a data-driven forward chaining system.

   Oracle's Rules Engine can work with Java programs and can be deployed independently or with an app server. Although Oracle literature talks about using Oracle Business Rules with the BPEL Process Manager and BAM, there is no documentation that shows seamless integration between these products.

   Oracle's Business Rule Language seems quiet different from Drools. Right now the Rules Language only includes if and else statements, i.e. they are Condition-Action rules. There is no details available on any upgrades and if they contain will contain events in the future.

3) Workflow: Oracle Workflow product that was integrated with the 9i app server has graduated into the Oracle BPEL Process Manager (part of Oracle SOA Suite) which can now be integrated into Websphere, Jboss and Weblogic app servers. The BPEL PM includes a Visual Designer (with Drag and Drop process modeler) and bindings for WS, JMS and JCA. The BPEL PM can

also expose a process flow as a Web Service (Can this WS be invoked by a consequent action of a Rules Engine? Probably yes).

BPEL PM follows the WS-BPEL standards and can be integrated with Databases, ESBs, Portals and SAP too. Oracles BPEL Server sits on a JEE app server and consists of a BPEL Engine, built-in integration services and WSDL Binding.

There is no information yet on how the BPEL PM product can be seamlessly integrated with the Rules Engine. From examples seen so far, all decision points (if-then conditions) seem to be written in BPEL statements only (using switch).

4) ESB: Oracle has an Enterprise Service Bus (ESB) as part of its 10g Application Server. The ESB provides features like Reliability, Data Transformations, adapters for connectivity, content based routing, etc.

   Oracle also has a light-weight bus called the Oracle Service Bus as part of its SOA Suite.

5) Orchestration: Oracle does not advertise an Orchestration product per se, but they can do Service and Workflow Orchestration with a number of products available as part of their SOA Suite (BPEL PM, ESB, Oracle Rules and Oracle Web Services Manager). They use the BPEL PM for assembling discrete services to create an end-to-end Workflow. To this Workflow they can add Business Rules and Decision Services. However, it is not yet clear how (and to what level) Oracle Rules integrates with the BPEL process. Whether the Rules are used for orchestrating the Process itself or for making decisions in a Web Service instantiation of a process is not clear. Either ways, there seems to be some intent to integrate Business Rules with the BPEL PM workflow.

1.2 Summary

As discussed above, Oracle is in a strong position to do dynamic workflow orchestration using the Business Rules, BPEL PM and ESB. Some more research (and probably some inside information) is needed to determine the level of integration that exists between the Rules Engine and the BPEL PM. We also need to find out what is on Oracle's roadmap regarding this. A single product, that does Dynamic Workflow Orchestration using BPEL PM and the Rules Engine, doesn't exist today (its up to the customer to integrate them), but it may very well be on the roadmap.

2. IBM

As one of the most popular BPM solutions, IBM's BPM suite is positioned as "an integrated set of role-based, SOA-enabled software that provides customers with the ability to design, execute, and optimize core business processes." It offers a choice of two Foundational Offerings, the IBM WebSphere Dynamic Process Edition and the IBM FileNet Active Content Edition. The Dynamic Process Edition includes Business Modeler, Business Service Fabric, and Business Monitor to address the SOA lifecycle activities involving modeling, process execution and deployment, and process monitoring and improvement. The FileNet Active Content Edition addresses customer scenarios mainly involving content, people and decisions. In addition, the Optional Extended Value Offerings provide complex event processing capabilities, advanced analytics, BPM repositories, accelerators, adaptors, and collaborative tools.

2.1 Product

1) Events: The current version of WebSphere Business Events Processing (BEP) is composed of Complex Event Processing (CEP) and Business User Interface (BUI). BEP extends the capabilities of CEP to support high volume of heterogeneous business event types from multiple sources and business events and complex patterns that occur in no particular time or order. The BUI offered in BEP handles frequent changes to event processing logic and provides an interface for business users to maintain the event processing logic when needed.

2) Rules: The existing Business Rules capabilities offered by the current WebSphere Process Server include Rule Sets (If/Then rules) as well as decision tables. A web client provides an interface where the parameters of these rules can be changed by a business user, in a way which a natural language specification of these rules (e.g. If the car is color <xxx> then the price is <yyy>) is allowed. More complex rules capabilities will be added through the integration of ILOG's JRules. By integrating ILOG JRules with WebSphere Process Server, it will enhance the WebSphere BPM solution with enterprise rule repositories, decision tree support, template editors, Web-based management tools, and rule simulation and testing capabilities.

3) Workflow: WebSphere MQ Workflow supports business process workflows that interact with both people and system. It automates and tracks business processes in accordance with business design and provides integration processes with support for human interactions. By its own definition, a workflow is a business process of certain process logic that requires the participation of an organization of all people that are involved with the support of an infrastructure (i.e., computers and programs). MQ Workflow is a workflow management tool that can be used to define and document processes; run the defined processes to support the people doing the work and automate activities that do not require human guidance (e.g. implement them as web services); and administer the workflows.

4) ESB: WebSphere Enterprise Service Bus (ESB) is a flexible connectivity infrastructure for integrating applications and services. It is responsible for routing of messages between services, converting transport protocols and transforming message format between requestor and service, and handling business events from disparate sources. The ESB is a mediation layer builds on WebSphere Application Server foundation to provide intelligent connectivity.

5) Orchestration: The WebSphere Services Fabric (WSF) builds on WebSphere Process Server (WPS) that builds on WebSphere ESB and WebSphere Application Server (WAS) foundation to deliver business process management. Within the WSF, policy-based orchestration capabilities are provided in the form of dynamic business assembly and delivery that is supported by binding services at runtime based on business context. The WPS offers process driven, choreography-alike capabilities to manage the life cycle of business processes, to navigate through the associated process model, and to invoke the appropriate Web services. The process choreographer also provides the appropriate quality-of-service (QoS) characteristics, such as maintaining a certain response time or ensuring particular security constraints.

2.2 Summary

IBM's offerings of Business Events, Business Process Management, and Rule management is defined as a future solution of event-driven SOA with a strong focus on an integrated, role-based, end to end business solution supported by advanced analytics.

In a long-term vision, rules can be and will be applied across different phases of SOA lifecycle and business rule management will be employed in a number of different capacities that are closely intertwined in the lifecycle. Beyond its current plans of integrating ILOG's JRules Engine with the WebSphere Process Server for improved management of policy-intensive processes and improved collaboration between developers and business users, IBM strategizes to provide a centralized repository of rules (ILOG) for an application that will likely work with Tivoli (a comprehensive portfolio of tools for system management) on runtime and work with their BPM suite on the design time and runtime for BPM, and on the build time with Rational.

The key differentiator here is distributed decision making. The WebSphere BPM offerings assume a centralized control point and a centralized intelligence repository for all types of governance that are needed in BPM for ED-SOA. Technically, it has a strong dependency on Web 2.0 technology and BPEL4WS.

The distinction between orchestration and choreography made by IBM WebSphere isn't necessarily reflected in its offerings. Although an authoritative distinction between these two is still lacking in the BPM community, there is a common agreement that both orchestration and choreography need to be employed for better service orientation. What IBM is offering is business rules based process orchestration at a coarse-grained level. For more complex processes that are highly dynamic, real choreography is needed for an autonomous component or element to dynamically adjust its behavior and interact with other processes to accomplish policy specified business goals – which is ultimately what our policy based solution will offer.

3. Red Hat

JBoss is a division of Red Hat that specializes in open-source middleware software. It provides a set of Java EE projects, including JBoss AS, Hibernate, Tomcat, JBoss ESB, jBPM, JBoss Rules (formerly Drools), JBoss Cache, JGroups, JBoss Portal, JBoss Seam, JBoss Transactions, and JBoss Messaging - all marketed under the JBoss Enterprise Middleware Suite (JEMS) brand.

3.1 Products

1) Events: Drools Fusion is a temporal reason system providing CEP capabilities. Events are now treated as first class citizens (a special type of facts) in the rules engine. It allows specification of event correlation and time based constraint using a number of time constraint operators (e.g., coincides, before, after, meets, metby, overlaps, overlappedby, during includes, starts, startedby, finishes, finishedby and sliding windows support). Fusion, however, is NOT a CEP engine for analyzing, detecting, correlating, abstracting and processing events.

2) Rules: Drools was originally designed as an enhanced rules engine implementation, and on top of it is a Business Rule Management System (BRMS). Drools is focused on a production rule approach – each rule is a "when-then" structure using first order logic for knowledge representation. The rule inference engine is implemented based on an extended Rete algorithm called called ReteOO (for object-oriented systems). *Guvnor* is their BRMS component that covers rule management, storage, editing and deployment through a web-based user interface. The latest version Drools (5.0) will be the launch of what they call the Business Logic integration Platform (BLiP) – the BRMS is dead. The FUTURE is for a unified and integrated solution for Rules, Processes and CEP.

3) Workflow: There are 2 workflow engines provided by JBoss:
   a. Drools Flow – Drools Flow is said to be a full-blown workflow and process engine that allows advanced integration of processes and rules. It is essentially (until now) an extended rules engine (based on Ruleflow) that allows one to specify the order in which rule sets should be evaluated by using a flow chart.
   b. jBPM – jBPM is a workflow management system that contains a "Process Virtual Machine" (PVM) – a generic engine for executing different process models. PVM contains a process model, a runtime model, API and a set of services that are useful for process language implementations (e.g., persistence, transaction management, etc.) BPEL, XPDL, jPDL and SEAM PageFlow are the four different process languages that are built on top of PVM.

4) ESB: JBossESB is an SOA infrastructure that supports:
   a. Messaging service including JBossMessaging, JBossMQ, MQSeries, OracleAQ, TibcoEMS and ActiveMQ
   b. Message Routing: Static and Content Based using Drools
   c. Message Transformation: Fragment based Data Transformation Engine

<ol type="a" start="4">
<li>XML Registry using the JAXR API</li>
<li>Persisted Event Repository</li>
<li>Base Transport Mechanism</li>
<li>Pluggable Architecture</li>
<li>Notification Service</li>
<li>Web services Support</li>
<li><u>jBPM Integration</u></li>
<li>Hot Deployment</li>
<li>Complex Splitting, Enrichment and Routing of Huge Messages</li>
</ol>

<ol start="5">
<li>Orchestration: Drools Ruleflow – there are several scenarios where rules can be used in the processes:
<ol type="a">
<li>Rules can be grouped in a Ruleflow group that is referenced by a RuleSet node in the workflow.</li>
<li>Rules can be attached to decision nodes for evaluating constraints</li>
<li>Assignment rules can be used to determine which actor is responsible to take action whenever a new human task needs to be executed.</li>
<li>Rules can be used for describing exceptional situations and how to respond to these situations.</li>
<li>Rules can be used to dynamically fine-tune the behavior of the process (e.g., new rules could be added at runtime to log additional information or handle specific cases of the process)</li>
</ol>
</li>
</ol>

(Future) Drools PVM+ extends PVM and allows integration of rules and processes: Processes can include (the power of) rules in their process model whenever appropriate, e.g. split decisions, assignment of actors to work items, rules as expression language, etc. vice-versa, rules can start processes during their execution. On top of PVM+ are Drools Flow and other flow languages.

3.2 Summary

The jBPM team and Drools team have been in conversation about integration for a couple of years. But the only support right now is limited to the invocation of rules from the jBPM ActionHandler, DecisionHandler or AssignmentHandler (which are way too low-level java code implementation). The Drools team believes in a unified rules and processes approach which the jBPM team doesn't buy, and they have never been able to reconcile this difference. For this reason, the Drools team sticks to its own workflow engine (Drools Flow). They don't plan to do the BPEL, BPM layers and instead hope the jBPM team will become the consumers of the Drools tech. Although Drools aims at a unified approach on rules and processes, it's still a long way to go because the current solution is too coupled to rules. In addition, they don't focus on dynamic orchestration (though they might have the capability to do so) and distributed decision making.

4. Microsoft

Microsoft's Windows Workflow Foundation (WF) provides a common foundation for workflow in Microsoft products and technologies. Microsoft's BPM Service offerings based on WF include Windows SharePoint Services (WSS) v3, BizTalk Server 2006, Windows Exchange Server and Office SharePoint Server 2007. Since these services are built on Windows Workflow Foundation (WF), we will focus on the WF for the analysis in this section.

4.1 Windows Workflow Foundation

In Windows Workflow Foundation (WF), a workflow is a set of activities. Each activity is actually a class that can be reused in multiple workflows. It ships with a set of general purpose activities for defining workflows in so-called Basic Activity Library (BAL). This base activity library provides the ability to define control flows using familiar constructs such as IF/ELSE and WHILE loops. Developers are also free to implement custom activities focused on a particular problem space. Therefore, the activity library can be provided by Microsoft or anybody else. Other basic activities provided include Sequence, Parallel, Code, Listen, Delay, FaultHandler, Compensate, CallExternalMethod, HandleExternalEvent, InvokeWorkflow, InvokeWebService, Terminate. They are similar to those of BPEL's activities but not exactly the same. In order to support BPEL, WF provides a BPEL Activity Library that implements BPEL 1.1. Workflows built with this library can be imported from or exported to BPEL. BizTalk Server 2006 also can import and export BPEL definitions.

WF provides three built-in workflow types: Sequential, State machine and Rules-driven Workflow. WF also provides options for defining workflows. Workflow designing can either be graphical using the Workflow Designer or directly writing code in C#, Visual Basic, or another .NET language.

Sequential workflow structures its activities into a pre-defined pattern like activities in flow chart. Developers specify what to do first, next, after that and last etc. In contrast, a state machine workflow organizes its activities into a finite state machine. It defines a group of states and events, which trigger transitions between these states. It uses a different set of basic activity library which includes the following. First, State: Represents a state in a workflow's state machine. Second, EventDriven: Defines a transition containing one or more activities that should be executed when a specific event is received while in a particular state. Third, SetState: Changes the state of the workflow's state machine. A transition might or might not change the workflow's state. Fourth, StateInitialization: Defines one or more activities that should be executed by default whenever a particular state is entered.

The third type of workflow, i.e. rule-driven workflow, is of particular interest to us. Microsoft considers handling business rules well in business process is very important, and thus it provides several approaches to integrate business rules into BPM. First of the approaches is called code condition. It directly adds business rules into workflow using activities like IfElse and While etc. However, this kind of rules can't change workflow at runtime. Second is so-called rule condition. In this approach, rule conditions are stored in an XML format in a separate file. Developers can directly write rule condition file or use a tool called Rule condition editor. The workflow will access the rule condition file for instruction. When a workflow reaches a rule condition, the condition's expression is evaluated for branching workflow activities. Unlike code conditions, rule conditions can be changed on-the-fly for a running workflow.

In addition, WF provides a rules engine that can be accessed through the Policy activity. Using this activity, a developer can define a group of rules called a *rule set*. Each rule has the form IF <condition> THEN <action> ELSE <action>. For example, an insurance company might create a Policy activity with a rule set containing all of its underwriting qualifications. Drivers under 21 might be ranked as high-risk, for example, unless they have good grades in school, while married drivers might be given a lower risk ranking. A workflow that needs to determine whether a particular applicant conformed to these rules could then invoke this Policy activity. The Windows Workflow Foundation rules engine would determine which rules in this rule set are true, and then execute those rules. This execution might change the state of the workflow in such a way that other rules in the rule set have now become true. To handle this, the rules engine examines and, if necessary, executes any affected rules in the rule set again, a technique known as *forward chaining*. This process continues until either no new rules become true or a predefined limit is reached.

Regarding ESB (Enterprise Service Bus), the only thing we found is that BizTalk Server 2004 and 2006 provides for all the capabilities of traditional ESBs. Also BizTalk Server delivers full support for business process, business activity monitoring, and business rules with built-in management and deployment of connected systems.

4.2 Summary

In summary, Microsoft WF does provide both a workflow engine and rules engine. The rules engine can be separate from the workflow engine and use business rules to control workflow. However, it only has limited dynamic workflow management capability. First, it is not event-driven business rule management. The rules are only evaluated at fixed points when the workflow reaches the pre-set activity point. Second, the workflow can not be dynamically composed. While policies can be changed and re-evaluated, the branches of workflows are pre-established and can't be changed at runtime.

5. TIBCO

TIBCO has been a major provider for Message Oriented Architectures since 1996 and is currently one of the major players behind IBM in this area. Although known for their Enterprise Service Bus (ESB) TIBCO has leveraged this expertise and transitioned into a Business Process Management (BPM) provider as well.

5.1 Products

1) Events: TIBCO BusinessEvents is TIBCO's event framework which collects, filters and correlates events. This support naturally leads to supporting CEP, and many analysts have given TIBCO praise in this area. The event framework uses a model-driven approach, which consists of a contextual model for capturing expected outcomes, a conceptual model to capture the static relationships, a state model to capture dynamic relationships and an aggregate model to capture the context of related events. The events feed into a RETE-Based rules engine that exists within the framework. TIBCO models their work after the Rapide event pattern language, a full-featured events and rules language of the form Event-Condition-Action (ECA).

2) Rules: As mentioned above, TIBCO BusinessEvents contains a rules engine, but TIBOC also provides other products that contain rules engine, specifically, TIBCO ActiveMatrix Policy Manager and TIBCO iProcess Decisions. The Policy Manager is meant specifically for security so it is not a focus at this time. However, iProcess Decisions is a critical part to their iProcess Suite that provides for rule based node in a process flow. The iProcess Decisions Studio is used to create and test rules, providing drag and drop functionality. Rules appear reusable among agents since they are stored in a Decisions Server.

3) Workflow: TIBCO iProcess Suite is a suite of application modules that has been designed to provide a complete end-to-end process management solution. There are a number of parts that exist to create the overall suite and is broken down into specific areas:

Modeling:	TIBCO	Business	Studio
Rules:	TIBCO	iProcess	Decisions
Goals:	TIBCO	iProcess	Conductor
Execution:	TIBCO	iProcess	Engine
Analysis:	TIBCO	iProcess	Analytics
Optimization:	TIBCO	iProcess	Insight

These pieces provide a strong product for PBM and workflow.

4) ESB: TIBCO ActiveMatrix Service Bus is their ESB product and is the product that most people associate with TIBCO. It is a lightweight enterprise service bus that enables organizations to

separate transport from services within their SOA infrastructure. There is a level of transparency provided by the bus in that any service hosted on the bus can change its location or communication protocol such that it is transparent to the end user.

5) Orchestration: There are no current products that provide for behavioral orchestration, where rules drive the workflow. However, nodes within their workflow do contain rules to find the current state of the system.

5.2 Summary

TIBCO's overall architecture is a distributed solution where agents are used to make decisions, avoiding a hub and spoke architecture. This could be used to support distributed decision making (DDM), however there is no mention of this in the current literature. TIBCO provides for all the pieces that are necessary to provide a similar solution that we are looking into. In some of their documentation they allude to some dynamic workflow ideas, however there is a not clear evidence that there solution is anything more than just a node that has rules in it.

6. Sun Microsystems

Sun has always been on the forefront of products related to Java and JEE based products. Sun has been responsible for authoring most of the specs related to Java and JEE and related technologies and products.

With respect providing a product that can do dynamic workflow orchestration, Sun seems to be missing the Rules Engine component of it. However, given Sun's involvement with the open source community, they are capable of using Drools or JBoss Rules to put together a product that can do dynamic workflow orchestration. The only question is whether it's in their roadmap.

6.1 Products

1) Events: As part of their CAPS platform, Sun provides an Intelligent Event Processor (IEP) and a Business Activity Monitor (BAM). The Intelligent Event Processor is capable of event filtering, aggregation, correlation and analysis across multiple applications. Complex Event Processing (CEP) capabilities are available as part of the BAM product.

2) Rules: Surprisingly, Sun does not seem to have a Rules Engine product. The Java CAPS suite has the capability to integrate with third party Rules Engine products, but Sun does not sell their own Rules Engine.

3) Workflow: Sun's Business Process Manager (BPM) is available as part of the CAPS suite. The BPM allows for process driven integration. It provides the ability to model, test, implement, monitor, manage and optimize business processes that orchestrate flow of activities across any number of Web Services, systems, people and partners. The BPM also has a graphical modeling environment for BPEL. Since Sun does not have a Rules Engine, they do not explicitly integrate the BPM solution with a Rules Engine. However, integration with a Rules Engine is possible using JBI.

4) ESB: Sun also provides an ESB called the Sun Enterprise Service Bus that uses the JBI (Java Business Integration) standard to allow components to communicate. The ESB is based on the open source Open ESB product for Sun Glassfish Enterprise Server.

5) Orchestration: Sun only seems to use the BPM product for orchestration and ESB for helping components communicate. Sun does not seem to be a big player in the BPM or the Rules Engine space. They seem to be trying to focus on Identity management and portals and are trying to use BPM for orchestration. It is not clear if they will come up with a product that uses does orchestration with Rules based decision points for control. Given Sun's proclivity to do everything in a standard manner and to rigorously follow standards, this appears unlikely.

6.2 Summary

As discussed above, Sun could build a product that does dynamic workflow orchestration, but given the fact that Sun does not own a Rules Engine and that they tend to focus more on standards, it's not likely that Sun will build one in the next 12 to 24 months.

7. SAP

SAP is the third major software vendor, after IBM and Oracle, which has architected a business process platform called "SAP NetWeaver Platform" on top of an ESB. SAP NetWeaver enables rapid but controlled business process change. The platform incorporates business functionality – exposed as ready-to-use enterprise services and process components – through its enterprise services repository. It also provides an integrated platform of composition technologies for orchestrating business processes, composing applications, and deploying solutions.

7.1 Products

1) Events:

    SAP NetWeaver Business Event Management (BEM) – BEM is the process of capturing real-time business events from multiple sources and assigning them to the appropriate decision-maker for resolution based on the business context of the events. This includes:

    a. Business activity monitoring – You can act on significant events or groups of events and take action in the right business context. With SAP NetWeaver, you can monitor, measure, and analyze the efficiency of your business processes.

    b. Business task management – You can get the right tasks to the right people so they can complete their tasks on time with the best results. With SAP NetWeaver, you can automate online processes, support offline processes, and coordinate access to tasks across the enterprise.

    Future release of SAP NetWeaver BRM (around 2010) will incorporate CEP capabilities to support rule-based responses to business events in real-time business scenarios like fraud detection, SLA monitoring, etc.

2) Rules:

    SAP NetWeaver BRM – With the acquisition of YASU Technologies (a privately held leader in BRM systems), SAP enhances its BPM offerings and provides customers with the agility they need to easily embed new business rules in business processes. Rules are in form of "if-then" or decision tables and can be written based on Java Classes or XML schema. BRM acts as an accelerator for BPM and improves efficiency through decoupling of decision logic from process logic, through capturing, automation and alignment of critical business rules and the decisions they drive as reusable services, as well as through rule-based correlations for real-time business events. SAP BRM consists of:

    a. Rules Composer: the modeling and implementation environment for business rules; it provides seamless navigation from business process to business rules through integrated modeling for processes and rules.

    b. Rules Analyzer: the environment for testing, refining, analyzing and optimizing business rules.

c. Rules Manager: a web based environment for modeling, editing and managing business rules by use of business users.

d. Rules Repository: provides rules versioning, permissions management, access control, alerts and other repository services.

e. Rules Engine: runtime for rules execution.

3) Workflow:

SAP NetWeaver BPM – building blocks are:

a. SAP NetWeaver Composition Environment: supports a standards-based modeling environment (OMG BPMN, Business Process Modeling Notation), process design collaboration, semantic integration with SAP's application core processes, human interaction management that provides task management, rule and responsibility assignments and business event resolution mechanisms.

b. Enterprise Services Repository: contains enterprise services (service interfaces, service operations) and data types but also tools to cover the integration needs of a SOA middleware (e.g., a mapping editor, a BPEL integration process editor)

c. SAP Enterprise Modeling Applications: contains a large scale of enterprise modeling projects, such as descriptive models, business process analysis, conceptual simulation/optimization, process planning & governance, process performance measurements, etc.

d. ARIS: a modeling environment for conceptual process planning and documentation - not "model-to-code". It comes with a BPEL "diagram type".

4) ESB:

SAP does not intend to provide a separate ESB offering. A lot of the capabilities provided by an ESB come with the NetWeaver platform. This confirms the current trend in the industry in "distributing" ESB capabilities onto the edges, at the services activation layer, rather than forcing all interactions to go through a central piece of infrastructure.

5) Orchestration:

In SAP, orchestration is referred to BPEL-based web service orchestration to automate how different business systems could be integrated with the help of an executable flow model.

7.2 Summary

SAP sees the future trend as convergence of various disciplines: BRM with BPM, Business Intelligence (BI) and CEP where BRM together with BPM become critical components of Enterprise SOA. In their implementation, rules are stored as part of the process model. They don't consider rule-driven dynamic workflow and distributed decision making.

8. Fiorano

Positioned as a leading provider of business process integration and messaging technology solutions, Fiorano offers an ED-SOA solution to support the integration and event-driven process orchestration among various applications and platforms including J2EE, .NET, Web services and legacy systems.

8.1 Product

1) Events: Although Fiorano targets at the event driven architecture, it does not offer any CEP capabilities. Fiorano uses the event-driven service model to enable services to be executed as independent entities and dynamically binds these entities for event driven process orchestration. The FioranoMQ product is a gird-enabled, peer-to-peer JMS messaging platform that mainly serves as a standalone messaging server for dynamic event routing, distributed debugging of event flows, invocation of JCA components, etc.

2) Rules: No rules component is offered by Fiorano.

3) Workflow: Because Fiorano focuses on the event-driven architecture, the workflows are virtually defined as event –flows between distributed services to be set up dynamically by the underlying middleware. Fiorano supports BPEL workflows and allows general-purpose applications, encapsulated in JCA containers, to be orchestrated in a standards-based manner.

4) ESB: Fiorano ESB supports both EDA and SOA, allowing a Business Component Architecture that encapsulates and integrates business functions across different platforms and languages to be built upon the ESB. Fiorano ESB supports multiple communication protocols, including SOAP/HTTP and JMS, together with Fiorano MQ to enable messages to be transferred between distributed business components. In addition, Fiorano ESB provides fault handling and performance improvement capabilities such as failover (at both server and business-component levels), load-balancing, security, monitoring and other management services using the JMX standard.

5) Orchestration: The Fiorano Process Orchestrator allows end-users to compose event-driven distributed business processes by synthesizing event-driven processes with loosely coupled components from J2EE, .NET, C/C++/Legacy applications and Web Services. The Fiorano ESB connects the services and enables configuration, selection, and dynamic modification of the services that participate in a distributed event-driven business process. The orchestrator can also serve as a centralized process engine that controls and monitors the data flow and intercepts events within a process.

8.2 Summary

Fiorano's offerings have a very strong focus on interoperability and integration technologies, including support for messaging, transformation and connectivity, routing, and service orchestration. Fiorano aims to provide a middleware solution that encompasses a comprehensive application and process integration and deployment capability for SOA using its Business Component Architecture (BCA) built over an ESB platform.

Fiorano does not offer any solution in the Business Rules Management domain. Nor does it plan to extend its current offerings to connect BPM and BRM.

9. Lombardi

Lombardi's business process management products include teamworks6, Blueprint and Process Definition Package and Process Deployment package. While teamworks6 is their main product for business process modeling and deployment, other products are accessories. Blueprint is for process documentation and process definition package and process deployment package have names explained their purpose. Lombardi products not only have all graphics based design tools but also have other rich and helpful features. It can help test, debug and suggest solution for problems. It has process optimizer to help to improve your process performance and live report to visualize your process execution.

Lombardi's graphic design tool allows you to easily enter rules as well. However, the rules are for routing process to different branches only. In addition, they embed rules into workflows but don't separate them, which limits them to static workflow management tool.

12 References

[1] Brian F. Chellas, Modal Logic. Cambridge University Press, Cambridge Massachusetts, 1980.

[2] Paul Harmon and Celia Wolf, "The State of Business Process Management - 2008", the BPTrends Report, February 2008. http://www.bptrends.com/surveys_landing.cfm

[3] Andy Dornan, "SOA: Convergence and Consolidation", InformationWeek Analytics, September 2007. http://i.cmpnet.com/v3.businessinnovation.cmp.com/pdfs/nwca_soa_report.pdf

[4] "Motorola Business Policy Language version 6.9.2", December 2007. http://compass.mot.com/doc/293297030/BPLv6.9.2.doc

[5] Microsoft Windows Workflow Foundation. http://msdn.microsoft.com/en-us/netframework/aa663328.aspx

[6] Microsoft Windows Workflow Foundation rule engine. http://msdn.microsoft.com/en-us/library/aa480193.aspx

[7] Drools User Guide. http://downloads.jboss.com/drools/docs/4.0.7.19894.GA/html_single/index.html

[8] VidSys information (introduction, white papers, manuals, presentations, demo, practices, training materials) from Internet

[9] NICE information (introduction, white papers, manuals, presentations, demo, practices, training materials) from Internet

[10] OnSSI information (introduction, white papers, manuals, presentations, demo, practices, training materials) from Internet

www.ingramcontent.com/pod-product-compliance
Lightning Source LLC
LaVergne TN
LVHW071523070326
832902LV00002B/56